LEADERSHIP:

FINDING YOUR
SWEET SPOT

Move from being a good leader to a
Great Leader!

Paul B. Thornton

AUTHORS PLACE
— PRESS —

Published by Authors Place Press
9885 Wyecliff Drive, Suite 200
Highlands Ranch, CO 80126
AuthorsPlace.com

Manufactured in the United States of America.

ISBN: 978-1-62865-692-3

CONTENTS

INTRODUCTION

What does it take to go from being a good leader to a great leader?

The right amount!

To grow healthy and happy plants, you need to provide the right amount of water, sunlight, fertilizer, and pruning. Too much or too little water will hurt your plants; too much or too little sunlight can cause plants to stop growing and die. The best gardeners learn what each plant needs to grow and blossom.

Similarly, leaders must find the right amount of coaching, direction, and empowerment to give each employee. Too much coaching can be as bad as too little coaching! Too much direction can be humiliating and demotivating, while too little direction creates confusion.

Aristotle made this point when he said, *"Anybody can become angry - that is easy, but to be angry with the right person and to the right degree and at the right time and for the right purpose, and in the right way - that is not within everybody's power and is not easy."*

Here are the big questions you need to ask yourself:

As a leader, do I consistently serve up the right amount of what's needed?

Do I serve it up at the right time?

FINDING YOUR LEADERSHIP SWEET SPOT

In sports, the "sweet spot" refers to the area on a racket or club that makes the most effective contact with the ball. Your "leadership sweet spot" is when your actions have the most positive impact. You do precisely what is needed to produce the best results.

In "The Zone: Evidence of a Universal Phenomenon for Athletes Across Sports," researchers defined the Ideal Performance State (IPS) as "...a state in which an athlete performs to the best of his or her ability. It is a magical and...special place where performance is exceptional and consistent, automatic and flowing. An athlete [can] ignore all the pressures and let his or her body deliver the performance that has been learned so well. Competition is fun and exciting."

"The Zone" study surveyed 59 athletes from a variety of sports concluding that the athletes performed best when they were in IPS. They felt confident, focused, and relaxed, even during intense pressure. When leaders operate in their sweet spot, they are also confident, focused, and perform at their best.

Finding your leadership sweet spot in each situation is challenging. Needs vary, and individual skills and experience are different from task to task. Motivation can change from day to day, and what one person sees as a challenge, another sees as a walk in the park.

Some leaders operate at the extremes—doing too much, then too little. They centralize, then they decentralize, only to centralize again. Some leaders delegate, but then swoop back in and grab control.

The best leaders learn to diagnose each unique set of circumstances and determine what's needed to improve the situation.

- ▶ Diagnostic skills include the following:
  - ▶ Asking the right questions
  - ▶ Making the right observations
  - ▶ Clarifying thoughts and emotions
  - ▶ Analyzing the data
  - ▶ Identifying what's working and what can be improved
  - ▶ Determining what attitudes and resources are needed to move forward

Doctors make diagnostic judgements prior to prescribing various medications and treatments. When symptoms and conditions change, doctors change their recommendations. Doctors follow a rational, systematic process to determine what will help the patient. The best leaders use a similar approach. They diagnose before taking action!

Leaders determine what changes are necessary and possible. They decide what is required to engage, energize, and empower people to change. And they make ongoing adjustments as conditions change.

The aim of this book is to help you (*coach, consultant, executive, middle-manager, mentor, parent, supervisor, teacher, and team-leader*) find your leadership sweet spot in each situation.

When you find your leadership sweet spot, the outcome is awe-inspiring! It's a *WOW*!

People say things like, *"Your guidance was perfect," "You nailed it," and "You did exactly what needed to be done."*

When you operate in your sweet spot, your performance goes from good to great.

You achieve the most positive results!

The book is divided into two parts:

- ▶ Part I: Finding the Right Spot
- ▶ Part II: Finding the Right Ratio

DEDICATION

To my family—

Mary Jean,

Kate and Corey,

Andrew and Jess,

and our amazing grandsons

Owen, Anthony, Noah, Keegan, and Dominic.

May you always operate in your sweet spot!

ACKNOWLEDGEMENTS

Special thanks to all the leaders who shared their insights regarding finding and operating in their leadership sweet spot.

PART I

FINDING THE RIGHT SPOT

Too Much————versus————Too Little

Are you doing too much or too little?

Where is the fine line?

Consultants and college professors often answer these questions with two simple words—*it depends.*

- ▶ How much direction should I provide? *It depends.*
- ▶ How much work should I delegate? *It depends.*
- ▶ How much coaching is needed? *It depends.*

Of course, the answer to these questions *depends* on the situation and the people involved. Each situation brings a unique set of problems and opportunities.

The context is crucial!

There is a long list of leaders who succeeded in one setting but failed in another. They didn't properly diagnose the new situation nor adjust their approach and style as needed.

Different circumstances require different approaches.

On a scale of 1-to-10, how adaptable are you to changing circumstances?

Finding your sweet spot is an ongoing process that requires you to make adjustments as you gain new insights.

Strive to become more aware of your thoughts, emotions, and actions in each situation. What's your standard approach to connecting, engaging, and inspiring others?

You must become a great student—both of yourself and of the people you are leading! Get to know others on a deeper level. Strive to understand what they are thinking and feeling.

Conduct regular check-in meetings with your team members to discuss their successes and setbacks. What's holding them back? What resources would help them excel?

Like all great coaches, you need to learn to read the situation and make quick decisions.

Finding your leadership sweet spot doesn't mean moderation in all things. Rather, it means doing what's most appropriate, including cranking up to the maximum setting if that is what the situation requires.

Will the same approach work in all situations? No, of course not!

Versatility and flexibility are key.

For each of the topics in this section, think about the typical approach you use. Are you making the desired impact? Are you delivering extraordinary results? Are you operating in your sweet spot?

CANDID AND DIRECT

Too Much————————versus————————Too Little

Do you provide the right amount of candor in each situation?

There are times when people need a gentle nudge; other times they need a slap in the face (not literally).

When you are candid and direct, you reach people.

When administering discipline or providing "tough love," you must be direct.

Too direct! That's really a dumb idea.

When you are overly candid and direct, you may cause the person to become defensive and shut down.

Sometimes it is be better to start by planting seeds and arousing curiosity.

Open the door with suggestions like these:

- ▶ What if we...
- ▶ I wonder what would happen if...
- ▶ Have you ever thought about...

Too Indirect! Maybe, your performance could be better.

Dancing around the issue is often a waste of time. Don't sugarcoat the message.

A good question to ask yourself is—*How direct do I need to be with this person in this situation?*

One person that you need to be brutally honest and candid with is yourself. Your internal monologue must be accurate, honest, and truthful.

Read on to find out how others have found their sweet spot.

What's your approach? Comments from the field.

"I try to get to know each individual. Each person is unique. That helps me determine how direct or indirect to be.

To start the day, I give a high five, so to speak, to all the employees in my area. Their body language gives me an indication if there are any work or personal issues. I offer to talk privately with anyone who may want to.

You have to be flexible in your approach. I have one manager who is overly direct—all the time. That inflexibility is limiting his career advancement."

—Al Kasper, President, Savage Arms

"It's important to be crystal clear on the task, deadlines, and what 'completed staff work' looks like. You need to get agreement on what "done" or "completed" means. People have different understanding of what certain words mean. Achieving a 'shared meaning' is critical.

Being "too direct" relates to tone. If you are coming across as condescending or treating people like they are stupid—that's not good. People will shut down or get aggressive.

Your sweet spot is achieved when your directness is totally focused on helping your team members become successful at accomplishing the task."

—Alden Davis, Founder, MyValueTree.com

"I'm candid with my team when it comes to both good performance and poor performance. If they did well, I want to make sure they know that I noticed it and that I appreciate what they did. Conversely, if they didn't do well, I'm going to let them know that, too... but the key I've found isn't to dwell on the mistake, and instead focus on how to get it fixed and prevent future issues.

Once I move to the forward-looking side of things, that's when the "planting seeds" part typically comes in. I want to solicit their ideas. If I have examples of actions I've taken in the past that worked (or didn't work) in similar situations, I'll share it with them. But I've found that if I want them to truly implement changes, getting their ideas and buy-in on solutions is imperative."

—Robert J. Parslow, CPA, CMA, Senior Director at a Fortune 100 Healthcare Company

Self-reflection

1. In what situations do you need to be more direct?
2. In what situations would a more indirect approach produce more positive results?
3. In what areas do you need to be more honest with yourself?

COACHING

Too Much————————versus————————Too Little

Do you provide the right amount of coaching in every situation?

Part of your job as a leader is to coach and mentor to help people become more effective and efficient.

Leaders have a growth mindset—they believe everyone has untapped abilities and the potential for growth.

The right amount of coaching gives people just enough information at the right time to set them up for improvement.

Too much coaching! He's like a helicopter parent.

Too much coaching can often feel like micro-managing and can frustrate employees' motivation.

Overly-coached employees often show little initiative and demonstrate a lack of ownership. They wait to be told what to do and then do just that.

When you are too helpful, you make people "less able." They never learn to solve problems and make decisions on their own.

Some leaders overcoach because they have a big ego. Their comments are more focused on impressing others with their knowledge rather than helping people.

Don't overcoach.

Too little coaching! He never provides any help or guidance.

At the other extreme, some leaders are absent when it comes to providing valuable advice and guidance. These leaders come across as distant and uncaring—out of touch. As a result, employees perform below their potential.

Timing is essential. Sometimes it's productive to let the person wrestle with a problem before you jump in and start coaching.

Take advantage of teachable moments—those times when people are most open and receptive to coaching. However, in just about every interaction with your employees, there are some mini-coaching opportunities to build their knowledge and skills.

A good question to ask yourself is—*How much coaching does the person need in this situation?*

Read on to find out how others have found their sweet spot.

What's your approach? Comments from the field.

"To determine how much or how little coaching is needed, I take steps to understand the challenges my employees face in doing their day-to-day work. In addition, I make it a priority to learn their strengths and weaknesses, how they perform under pressure, and what motivates them.

I tailor my coaching to each individual. Some people need constant coaching and guidance, while others are independent, eager to learn, and task driven. Everyone is different.

I've learned it's important to stay flexible. As people grow and change for better or worse, the amount and type of coaching needed also changes. Focusing on the quality and timeliness of coaching, rather than how much or how little coaching to provide, has proven helpful in finding the right balance."

—*Michael Lambert, Team Leader*

"Micro-management" as a perfectionist is non-productive. "Micro-management," better called 'Micro-coaching or training' is a good thing; break things down into bite-size steps as a form of development. There are times when you need to closely monitor results until you know the person understands all the steps and actions required to produce the desired results. Then you can back off the amount of monitoring you're doing.

The sweet spot is achieved by knowing and supplying what the person needs to get the task done and meet all the requirements."

—*Alden Davis, Founder, MyValueTree.com*

"I think it is important to ask permission to coach. If the recipient isn't open, he or she will not benefit. *"Would you mind if I made a suggestion?"* *"Are you open to hearing another idea on how you might consider approaching the problem?"*

—Judy Zaiken, Corporate Vice President, LL Global, Inc.

Self-reflection

1. Are there situations where you provide too much coaching?
2. In what situations would it be beneficial to provide more coaching and mentoring? What actions will you take?

COLLABORATING

Too Much————versus————Too Little

Do you engage in the right amount of collaboration?

Collaboration requires a willingness to work together to develop innovative, win-win solutions. It requires trust and openness.

A lot of collaboration occurs during meetings especially when cross-functional teams meet.

Too much collaboration! We collaborate on everything!

Some leaders overdo it. They want to collaborate on every problem and issue that arises. This results in long discussions and multiple meetings—it's a time-killer!

Certainly, there are times when collaboration is useful. There are other times when you need to be assertive and make quick decisions.

Do you ever engage in too much collaboration?

Too little collaboration: "No input needed; here's my decision."

Some leaders think any collaboration is a waste of time. Their attitude is, *"I'll make the decision."*

Strong silos often lead to little or no collaboration across the organization!

People want to be involved and have a say on important issues.

Be selective as to when to collaborate and who you include in the discussion. Insightful customers, suppliers, and specific experts may be able to provide valuable contributions.

Some questions to ask yourself:

▶ Will collaboration improve the result?

▶ Is collaboration worth the time and effort?

Read on to find out how others have found their sweet spot.

What's your approach? Comments from the field.

"Collaboration is important to keep the team engaged, but the fine line is knowing how much is healthy and productive. I know I'm over-collaborating when the team becomes less efficient. There is a point when too much communication disables the decision workflow. Decisions don't get made in a timely manner.

And, I know I'm not doing enough collaborating when the team is less effective because an individual or department wasn't included in the discussion and analysis. At times, we all get into a "silo" mentality. I try to always keep the big picture in mind and include all the relevant people. The challenge is knowing how much collaboration is needed and who should be involved."

—Phil Goncalves, Senior Vice President
Commercial Lending, Country Bank

"Certainly, collaboration is a good thing. But sometimes a heated conversation is what's most needed. Some people have strong feelings that need to be expressed. To get to the core issues, you need to get the emotions out. Too much playing 'nice/nice—let's all get along' isn't the answer."

—Alden Davis, Founder MyValueTree.com

"When I'm fighting for the last word, instead of fighting to <u>find common ground,</u> nobody wins. When the conversation becomes more about me and less about problem-solving, nobody wins. When ideas take a back seat to ego, nobody wins."

—Molly Page, Freelance Writer and Digital Strategist

Self-reflection

1. Is more collaboration needed on certain issues?
2. What new voices might make your collaboration more effective?
3. In what situations would less collaboration be beneficial?

CONFIDENCE

Too Much————————versus————————Too Little

Do you always have the right amount of confidence in each situation?

The best leaders are confident in themselves and those they are leading.

We want to follow leaders who believe in themselves and their mission.

Confident leaders draw people to them.

Overconfident! I can do anything!

Some leaders think they can walk on water.

Overconfident leaders appear arrogant and cocky. They think they are invincible, so they take risks that aren't prudent. This is not smart!

When things go wrong, blaming others is a common response of the overconfident leader.

Lacking confidence! I'm not sure...well... maybe. I guess we could.

Leaders who lack confidence are hesitant, indecisive, and unwilling to make tough decisions. These leaders are overly concerned with being accepted and liked. They are willing to modify their position just to be accepted by others. This is not an effective way to lead!

Are you confident in your abilities? The more knowledge and skills you acquire, the more confident you will feel. The more prepared you are, the more confident you feel.

The right amount of self-confidence gives you peace of mind. You know what to do and have the courage to do it.

Do you believe in yourself and the people you are leading?

Read on to find out how others have found their sweet spot.

What's your approach? Comments from the field.

"Overconfidence in small doses is useful. It enables you to stretch yourself. Overconfidence – in large doses – is deadly."

—Dan Rockwell, Leadership Coach
and Author of the

"Confidence is an experiential-based trait that increases as you expand your comfort zone through consistent action. Confident leaders instill their vision in their teams and highlight the importance each brings through their individual strengths, thus, creating room for deeper collaboration and commitment. When leaders act with confidence, they are clear on their end goal and open to the path that will bring the best solution.

Overly confident leaders function more like dictators, forcing things to be done their way, leaving no room for collaboration or the input from their team members. While they may achieve their goal—in the long run—all they have done is create robots out of their direct reports. No innovation created, no loyalties developed, and no higher recognition for the team...all of which makes the next initiative harder to achieve."

—Belinda Pruyne, CEO
Business Innovations Group

"How much confidence is needed? It's situational. There are times when leaders need to have bravado to lift the energy of the group. There are other times when it makes sense for the leader to be humble—take more of a supportive role such as facilitator.

Confidence level is a variable I can control. I try to diagnose each situation and determine what's going to be most helpful to move the group in the right direction.

The sweet spot varies from situation to situation."

—Frank Deane, CEO, Lumleian, LLC

"Having enough self-confidence to be bold and create the life you want: good.

Using self-confidence as a shield against uncomfortable reality: bad.

Being so genuinely self-confident that you can say, 'Maybe I'm wrong' or 'I'm no longer sure...': priceless."

—Erica Andersen, Author, Speaker, and
Founding Partner of Proteus

Self-reflection

1. In what situations are you over-confident?
2. In what situation do you lack confidence? Why is that? What actions will you take to build your confidence?

COMPASSION

Too Much————————versus————————Too Little

Do you always provide the right amount of compassion and forgiveness?

The best leaders establish clear expectations and hold people accountable for completing tasks, meeting deadlines, and living the company values.

They also try to get a full understanding of what happened when things go wrong. They provide the right amount of compassion and forgiveness.

We want leaders who have empathy; leaders who can step into our shoes and understand our world.

Too much compassion! You're forgiven! You're forgiven!

Too much compassion equates to letting people off the hook. Always overlooking performance shortfalls allows people to continue being irresponsible. This is not a positive trait in a leader!

Some leaders think that they are being "nice and kind" by repeatedly showing their compassion. Too much compassion hurts people.

Too little compassion! No excuses! No mercy.

Some leaders have no compassion. They have no willingness to listen to any reason for delays, missed deadlines, or cost overruns.

They often hold grudges and never let go of past mishaps.

Certainly, there are times when some compassion is appropriate. There are extenuating circumstances. At times, people deserve a second, and maybe even a third chance.

It's important to consider the key factors in each case. What's the pattern? Does the person act like a victim, always blaming others? Or is this type of performance very unusual?

The right amount of compassion helps the person retain their self-esteem and learn from the experience.

Read on to find out how others have found their sweet spot.

What's your approach? Comments from the field.

"The boundary between too much and too little compassion makes itself apparent when you find people who complain too much or give excuses for poor performance. That usually is a sign of a wrong hire or someone with incorrect expectations. Such situations need to be corrected on a case-to-case basis, rather than reducing one's overall compassion. The default option--be as empathetic as you can, until you are proven wrong."

---Rostow Ravanan, CEO & MD, Mindtree

"We're all human beings. If I've got an employee with something major going on in their personal life, how focused are they going to be on their work? At the same time, the job's got to get done. So, where's the balance?

The best I've found is setting expectations right up front. I tell my team from the get-go to not schedule personal events, like vacations, during our busy periods. If an emergency pops up and they need to go, then I and the rest of the team pitch in to get the job done. What I've found is that my team understands that it's okay to be human, but not okay to take advantage of the rest of the team.

What happens when personal issues impact the long-term performance, the job getting done, and perhaps the rest of the team? At that point, it's time for a very candid discussion with that employee (and maybe even HR) to determine the right path forward. There's no easy answer to that one, but as the leader, it's up to you to make the ultimate call."

---Robert J. Parslow, CPA, CMA, Senior Director at a Fortune 100 Healthcare Company

"Compassion – where do I draw the line? I'm an overly compassionate person until I feel someone is taking advantage of me. Then I sometimes go the other direction and show little or no compassion. The sweet spot of providing the exact right amount of compassion varies from case to case. The art of being an effective leader is providing the right amount of compassion that will help the person learn from the experience and be more responsible and resourceful in the future."

---Karen Martin, President, TKMG Inc. (Author, and Consultant)

Self-reflection

1. In what situations do you need to show more understanding and compassion?
2. In what situations do you need to be firm and hold people accountable for results?

DECISIVE

Too Much————versus————Too Little

Are you decisive? Are you too decisive?

A big part of being a leader is making decisions in a timely manner.

Effective leaders are noticeably decisive on issues that relate to their core beliefs, values, and top priorities. They don't have to take a survey to figure out what to say or do.

You demonstrate your character when you make bold decisions that support your values.

Effective leaders also know when they must make a quick decision and when there is time to collect and analyze data before making a decision.

Too decisive! I don't need any data. We're going with Option A.

Sure, leaders need to have a "bias for action," but can you make decisions too quickly? Certainly!

Some leaders don't collect or analyze the relevant information before making a decision. This is not an effective way to proceed.

If you have expertise in the subject area, it may make sense to go with your gut. Otherwise, data is helpful.

Indecisive! I need a lot more data.

Indecisive leaders have difficulty deciding or sticking with their decision. They always want more data, more analysis, and more discussion.

A good question to ask yourself is—*Am I productively using all the data I have?*

Not making decisions brings teams and organizations to a halt. It's frustrating and demoralizing.

Leaders are indecisive for a variety of reasons, including lack of confidence and fear of failure.

When you operate in your "decisive sweet spot," you maximize your effectiveness. You make the best decisions within the allotted timeframe.

Read on to find out how others have found their sweet spot.

What's your approach? Comments from the field.

"I have had significant experience in the magazine business, more than 25 years. I am decisive on all issues related to my area of expertise, but we do live in a constantly changing world. So, there are times when I need to slow down a bit and gather more data before making a decision.

Indecision is a problem. Some leaders fear failure. They don't want to make a mistake or let the group down.

In my world of publishing, there are lots of deadlines, which means I'm forced to make decisions. If you find yourself being indecisive, I suggest you set your own deadlines. Put them in writing either on paper or on the calendar on your phone, tablet, or computer: *I will make a decision by 5:00 pm Friday on the ABC project.* Tell a colleague and ask him or her to hold you accountable.

Making the wrong decision isn't the end of the world, as long as you learn from it."

---Lorri Freifeld, Editor-in-Chief, Training Magazine

"A leader who is decisive is willing to take risks. Some leaders believe that if they look at all the data, understand all the contingencies, and calculate all the potential problems, the right decision will magically appear. However, when leaders attempt to do all the analytics, many develop "analysis paralysis" and are unable to make a decision. It is good for leaders to analyze data, look at trends, and anticipate problems. However, eventually, leaders need to take a risk and make a decision. When leaders recognize that most decisions are risks, they also acknowledge that they might make the wrong one."

---Joseph Folkman, founder of two leadership development firms: Novations and Zenger Folkman

"Everybody's got an opinion. Leaders are paid to make a decision. The difference between offering an opinion and making a decision is the difference between working for the leader and being the leader."

---Bill Walsh, former NFL Coach

Self-reflection

1. In what situations do you need to be more decisive?
2. When do you need to slow down and take time before making a decision?

DELEGATING

Too Much————————versus————————Too Little

Are you an effective delegator?

The ability to delegate the right tasks, to the right people, at the right time is a critical skill for every leader.

The benefits of effective delegation include:

▶ Empowering and developing your employees

▶ Establishing clear accountability

▶ Freeing up your time

Too much delegation! I'll assign it to Kate; I know she'll get it done!

Some leaders over-delegate to their superstars. They know their A-performers will do a great job and hit the ball out of the park. The danger of this approach is employee burnout. Even worse, your top performers may start resigning and move to your competition.

To prevent over-delegating, create a chart to track what you have delegated to each person. Remember, even superstars have limits!

Too little delegation! Check with me before you do anything.

Are you a control freak?

Some leaders think they must be directly involved with every problem and every decision. They may not trust their employees, or their ego longs to feel appreciated and valued.

When you under-delegate, you become the bottleneck in your operation. You stop developing your staff—not good!

Some employees want a shot at bigger projects and increased responsibility. Give these employees bigger bricks to carry.

The more you delegate, the more it frees up your time to work on bigger issues such as strategic thinking, organizational alignment, and long-term planning.

Of course, there are some things you should never delegate, including giving negative feedback to a direct report, pulling the plug on a major initiative, and announcing layoffs.

Where is the fine line? The right amount of delegation encourages employees to stretch and promotes creativity. However, too much delegation may thrust your employees into the anxiety-riddled panic zone.

However, the complexity of the tasks you delegate to employees, changes as they gain skills and experience.

Read on to find out how others have found their sweet spot.

What's your approach? Comments from the field.

"The boundary between over-delegation and under-delegation is generally discovered only on a case-to-case basis. If the person you have delegated to doesn't complete the task within the expected time-frame and/or with the desired quality, you know you have hit a roadblock. Until such a situation arises, it is better to delegate.

In my experience, I have found that more delegation is generally better for two reasons. The first is that it allows the team that reports to you to learn and grow as they take more responsibility. The second is that it frees up your time to take up higher-value tasks which leads to your growth."

---*Rostow Ravanan, CEO and MD, Mindtree*

"I had a tendency to over-delegate to the top performers who were also the most in demand. The probability of success was dramatically increased when delegating to Vinnie, Sue, or Michelle. I learned some subordinates like to be the go-to person. They like the challenge as well as the rewards and recognition. However, they had a breaking point. My insight is twofold:

1. When you delegate to your top performers, you have to have a relationship in which they feel comfortable to say – "ENOUGH." I had to be OK to hear that.

2. I had to either adjust their priorities, offer them additional resources, or assign some of their work to someone else. It also forced me to be very clear on my top priorities.

There were times when I under-delegated. I thought I was the only one who could do a specific task. I became too invested in the task outcome...when this happened, I may have produced the end product, but it may not have been the best outcome. In addition, my overly aggressive ownership of the task made it difficult for others to buy into the implementation.

Under-delegating, as I have described, also kept the light on me, rather than shining it on others."

---Mary Jean Thornton, former Senior Executive at The Travelers, and Professor of Business Administration

Self-reflection

1. Do you over-delegate to certain people?
2. In what situations could you increase what you are delegating?
3. What actions can you take to be a more effective delegator?

DISCUSSING

Too Much————versus————Too Little

Where do you fall on this spectrum?

Certainly, the amount of discussion needed on a specific topic is influenced by several factors such as priority, complexity, people involved, and time constraints.

Great discussions require great questions and an open and honest approach by all parties.

The best leaders ask questions that get to the core of the issue or opportunity. They ask questions that unravel complexity and simplify the options.

Too much discussion! Let's talk about it and it takes three hours.

Some leaders grant too much time to conversations that should take five minutes.

We've all been in meetings where it seems like the discussion goes on and on. The same themes are repeated over and over, and no one can bring closure to the agenda item. In some meetings, more time is spent complaining about the problem rather than trying to solve the problem.

Too little discussion! Let's move on!

On the other hand, some leaders cut the debate off too quickly. This results in people not feeling heard and not buying into the decision or plan.

Some leaders avoid discussing the elephant in the room; they don't want to bring up the tough, controversial issues. The best leaders know the "elephant" must be discussed.

The right amount of discussion begins with identifying the critical questions that need addressing and ends with a decision. Find the right balance between not wasting time and providing ample opportunity for people to weigh in and state their views.

Try adding some structure to the discussion.

- ▸ We have 20 minutes to discuss this issue, but then we must make a decision.
- ▸ Let's go around the table. Each person has 2 minutes to make their case, then we will make a decision.

Read on to find out how others have found their sweet spot.

What's your approach? Comments from the field.

"Discussion is a healthy way of getting "buy-in" from the group as a whole. However, sometimes I have to cut off the individual who talks too much in order to avoid not losing the commitment of the entire group. I try to get the quiet people involved. My goal is to have a healthy sharing of opinions, so all team members have a vested interest in the decision we make. It's important to hear all viewpoints, but also make timely decisions. It's a judgment call as to when to close the discussion and move to decision."

---Bill Condon, Vice President of Payroll, CBS

"Long discussions often arise when people are not prepared. People who have done their homework are clear and able to make their points simply and quickly."

---Kate Dinobile, college student and former Bank Specialist at Sberbank of Russia

"Good leaders will bring up the 'elephant' in the room. Poor leaders keep it under the rug and it just keeps getting bigger and bigger. When you avoid a conflict, people get stressed, annoyed, and start to question everything.

When I discuss the 'elephant' with a group or individual, I give them a heads-up notice—*We'll be discussing XYZ at tomorrow's meeting.* That gives them time to prepare.

At the meeting, it's critical to establish a few rules of engagement such as:

► Listen

► Don't interrupt

► Show respect

► A decision will be made

If people don't follow the rules, end the meeting. I have had to end two meetings because an individual wouldn't listen and constantly interrupted other to defend himself. Ending the meeting sends a powerful message.

Once a decision is made a few things need to happen:

1. Accountability—the person has to do what he has stated he will do. The leader needs to follow-up and check in on an agreed upon action.

2. The leaders should also look for changes in the person's behavior and let the person know when they see it. Reward and recognize effort and results.

3. The leader herself may need to make some behavioral modifications to address the elephant – good leaders aren't afraid to own things, get their hands dirty, and exemplify what they feel needs to change in others.

Discussing the elephant in the room isn't easy but necessary. It's messy and doesn't always go as planned."

---Kate Labor, Vice President of Sales, System and Software

Self-reflection

1. In what situations would more discussion be beneficial?

2. What topics or issues aren't being discussed that need to be discussed?

3. How do you know when it's time to bring closure to a discussion?

ESTABLISHING METRICS

Too Much————————versus————————Too Little

Do you have the right number of metrics for your team and organization?

Metrics drive behavior. What's measured gets people's attention. The metrics that are discussed in meetings further reinforce what's important.

What should be measured? Certainly, the financials. But what else?

The balanced scorecard approach developed by Robert S. Kaplan and David P. Norton recommends an approach of measuring customer and employee satisfaction, key business processes, as well as the financials. This allows you to get a balanced, well-rounded view of what's happening.

But here's another approach that worked. In this case, there was only one metric that got the focus.

In October 1987, Paul O'Neill gave his first speech as CEO of Alcoa, the aluminum manufacturing giant. He stated, "I want to talk to you about worker safety." Investors were eager to hear about profit margins, revenue projections, plans for reorganization, etc. Worker safety wasn't high on their list.

O'Neil knew many changes were needed but he felt he couldn't simply order people to change. Instead, he decided to start by focusing on one thing—<u>worker safety</u>. If he could start changing people's behaviors around one thing, it would spread to other processes and work practices throughout the entire company.

For the new CEO, safety trumped profits. The emphasis on the worker safety metric made an impact. During O'Neill's tenure, the number of lost work days due to injury dropped from 1.86 to 0.2.

However, there is more to the story. That impact extended beyond worker health. One year after O'Neill's speech, the company's profits hit a record high. Focusing on that one critical metric created a change that rippled through the whole culture.

Too many metrics! We track 35 variables on our dashboard.

The more metrics, the better! Not true!

If you don't know what's important, you tend to measure everything. Measuring unnecessary metrics produces piles of worthless data.

A focus on too many metrics splinters employees' attention and scatters their behavior. There are no clear-cut priorities when 35 metrics are being tracked.

Too few metrics! Just look at EBITA! (Earnings before interest, taxes, depreciation, and amortization.)

If you are only measuring the financials, you are looking at an incomplete picture.

You need to track a few key metrics to get the full picture of what's happening. It is useful to measure leading indicators, process performance, and results.

- Leading indicators—early activities that influence the production of products and services
- Process performance—how well the process is working
- The results—what's produced and how do customers respond to your products and services

When you measure a few things that really matter, you provide focus and clarity for the organization.

Read on to find out how others have found their sweet spot.

What's your approach? Comments from the field.

"We focus on having 3-to-5 metrics. The question we like to ask is, 'What are the critical metrics that will help improve the process or operation?' Metrics should focus on ways to improve the operation.

Whatever metrics you use, they should be simple, updated, and discussed on a regular basis."

---Al Kasper, President, Savage Arms

"When I work with clients to establish leading metrics, the question that we always discuss is - what is the one thing that you can control that will influence the desired results?

We try to keep the amount of metrics for an organization to 12-to-15 and like to keep individual metrics to 1-to-3. Keep it simple and focus on the critical few. We want to have our team members focused on driving what is the most important."

---Michael Vann, Senior Consultant, The Vann Group, LLC

"It's important for leaders to not only clearly state their vision, but also have a few metrics that indicate you've arrived. You need two or three metrics that relate directly to the achievement of your vision."

---Alden Davis, Senior Founder MyValueTree.com

Self-reflection

1. How many metrics do you focus on?
2. Are your metrics aligned with your top priorities?
3. Do you have the right balance of metrics that track leading indicators and the achieved results?

GAINING AGREEMENT

Too Much————————versus————————Too Little

How quickly does your team reach agreement on important decisions?

Top leaders work with their teams and gain agreement on the big items, including mission, vision, values, strategy, structure, and systems.

Too much agreement! We all think that's a great idea.

We all agree! Is that really a problem?

Total agreement may indicate "groupthink;" people are afraid to speak up and offer ideas.

When groupthink occurs, people go with the flow even when they disagree. Group harmony—*let's all get along*—is more valued than healthy dialogue and debate.

If there is too much agreement, you need to play devil's advocate—ask probing questions, challenge the current view, and encourage people to offer different ideas.

Too little agreement! No one agrees with the goal or plan.

At the other extreme, what if there is no agreement on important issues and goals?

This is a serious problem. Little progress occurs when everyone has a different agenda.

As a leader, you need to ask "why" and try to figure out what is going on. Have team members become firmly polarized?

Is there a lack of willingness to compromise or find common ground? Do certain team members need to be replaced? Does the whole team need to be disbanded and a new team charted?

Too much and too little agreement can be problematic.

You want healthy discussion and debate, but you also want to resolve differences, get closure, and commit to a specific course of action.

Read on to find out how others have found their sweet spot.

What's your approach? Comments from the field.

"Groupthink does happen. Some people hold back from sharing their ideas or opinions because they fear if their idea is accepted, they will be told to make it happen. They think: *More work for me!*

I work virtually, so I lead a lot of conference calls. Sometimes it's difficult to determine if groupthink is occurring during a call. One technique I use to encourage discussion is to ask people to be prepared to offer one to three ideas on a particular topic during the call.

Many ideas may be discussed, but at some point, you need to select the one or two that make the most sense. At this point, I shift the focus and say, *"Let's focus on Bob's idea. What has to happen to make that work and how can some of the other ideas we've discussed be applied to Bob's idea?"*

Getting all team members to accept and support the plan isn't always easy, but it's necessary."

---*Lorri Freifeld, Editor-in-Chief,* Training Magazine

"I teach courses on entrepreneurship and innovation where there is a significant amount of teamwork. I find that too much agreement gets in the way of innovation. You want a little tension and different viewpoints to spark healthy debate.

It's also important that the introverted team members have a say. Everyone needs a voice. Dominant personalities can force 'groupthink' to occur. When I see that happening, I play the devil's advocate and facilitate the discussion to get other ideas on the table.

Some of my student teams appear to be working fairly well, but when it's time to present and defend their ideas, things fall apart. The team never had full agreement on the product or the strategy they were proposing.

Leaders need to make sure all team members see the benefits of and support the team's goals and plans."

---*Diane Sabato, Professor of Business Administration and Small Business Owner*

Self-reflection

1. How do you prevent groupthink from occurring?
2. In what situations would more debate and discussion be beneficial?
3. What do you do when team members are firmly polarized on important issues?

MONITORING PERFORMANCE

Too Much————————versus————————Too Little

Do you monitor the right things at the right frequency?

Monitoring performance includes direct observation of what's happening, as well as getting verbal updates and written status reports.

Too much monitoring! I'll be back in 12 minutes to get a status update.

Some leaders micromanage their staff.

It's suffocating, it demotivates people, and it's a blow to their self-confidence.

In addition, constant monitoring is costly and time-consuming.

Too little monitoring. I didn't know that was happening!

At the other extreme, when leaders do insufficient monitoring, they are out of touch with what's happening. This is not good!

It's important to get out of your office and spend time speaking directly with employees and customers. Observe what they do and don't do. When problems occur, it's useful to go and see for yourself what happened.

What's the right amount of monitoring?

It depends on the priority and complexity of the task, as well as the capability of the person doing the task. You also need to adjust the amount of monitoring you're doing as conditions change.

Implementing major changes requires significant monitoring to see if the new behaviors and work procedures are taking hold.

The right amount of monitoring at the right time provides opportunities to make course corrections as needed.

Read on to find out how others have found their sweet spot.

What's your approach? Comments from the field.

"I think of monitoring as thinking forward to the end result, and then working backwards to determine how often I'll need a status update. For example, if I've got a team working on a project that's due in four months, I'm going to want a status update from them probably every two weeks. I've used weekly updates where there's enough happening each week to warrant the update, but weekly updates need to be 30 minutes at the absolute most. I've even done "daily huddles" (typically 5-10- minute gatherings, not even in a conference room) when times were crazy when the focus was just on what's due that day and who needs help in getting it done. I don't over-formalize the status updates, but it's critical to know if the team is off track and what they need from me to get them back on track. Beyond the project-based items, I typically hold team meetings once or twice a month just so everyone can hear what everyone else on the team is working on, and I can share with everyone what my focus areas are."

---Robert J. Parslow, CPA, CMA, Senior Director at a Fortune 100 Healthcare Company

"There are only three measurements that tell you nearly everything you need to know about your organization's overall performance: employee engagement, customer satisfaction, and cash flow. It goes without saying that no company, small or large, can win over the long run without energized employees who believe in the mission and understand how to achieve it."

---Jack Welch, Author and former Chairman and CEO of General Electric

"I lead a medical sales organization. I have 6 direct reports and a total group of about 70 people.

One of my key operating principles is –*'Inspect what you expect.'*

I monitor both performance and activities. Performance refers to the quantified metrics that are assigned to each of my direct reports. These are monitored weekly, monthly, and quarterly.

I also monitor activities. This relates to the sales funnel idea: are all the right front-end activities being done that lead to sales?

Monitoring is important and so is providing useful feedback.

Leading is both an art and science. The science relates to the metrics. Are they being achieved? Yes or no! That's easy. The art of leading is communicating and providing feedback so it is accepted, useful, and actionable. Each person is unique. You need to tailor your approach—that's an art.

I tell my direct reports the following: *'The rules need to be the same for everyone. But the way you deliver the message needs to be focused on the person.'"*

---Fred Kelly, Area Vice President of Sales, Masimo Corporation

Self-reflection

1. What situations require closer monitoring?
2. What situations require less monitoring?
3. Do you adjust your level of monitoring as situations change?

OPEN

Too Much————————versus————————Too Little

Are there situations when you are either too open or too closed?

Over the past few years, there has been a lot of buzz about the need for leaders to be transparent.

Authentic leaders are not afraid to state their views and show emotions when discussing setbacks and challenges they are facing. They tell people what they truly think and feel.

Open leaders are emotionally intelligent. They are able to control their emotions and communicate their message in a professional manner.

Leaders who are open make a positive connection with people!

Too open! I'll tell you whatever you want to know.

Leaders who are too open reveal all their doubts, fears, and insecurities. They risk losing credibility in the eyes of their followers.

In addition, some leaders are excessively open about their personal lives. They have no boundaries. This creates problems.

Too closed! That's none of your business!

Some leaders come across as cold and distant. They hide in their office and have little interaction with employees.

People want to know that their leader is a real human being.

Yes, there is a fine line between being too open and too closed, so be clear on what you are willing to share about the business and your personal life. Know your boundaries!

Let people get to know you as a person, but it's also important for them to understand you have limits as to what you will share.

Read on to find out how others have found their sweet spot.

What's your approach? Comments from the field.

"I prefer the word accessible. Having open communications helps build trust. Trust builds when you listen to people's ideas and concerns.

I also hold regular 'town-hall meetings.' I tell all employees the good and the bad things that are happening. I always try to be honest and straightforward."

---Al Kasper, President, Savage Arms

"On a personal basis, leaders must be approachable and display their humanness. When a leader has too high boundaries, employees are distanced from her and the business. Employees feel disconnected and view the leader as self-serving. If employees do not feel some connection to the leader, their connection to the business may be severed. Conversely, leaders must have boundaries when it involves relationships, information sharing, and resource allocation. The leader must be focused on fair treatment of all stake-holders, sharing critical information based on the principle of sharing with those on a "needs to know" basis, and supporting resource allocation decisions based on the needs and drivers of the business, rather than relationships."

---Mary Jean Thornton, former Senior Executive at The Travelers, and Professor of Business Administration

"The culture of an organization plays a part in how open or closed leaders are. I lean towards the 'very open and transparent' side. For me, *open* means being candid and direct. I try to drop the buzz words and give employees the candid, not 'BS' view of what's happening. This builds trust and strengthens my relationship with my employees."

---Neil Altieri, Director, New Business and Underwriting, MassMutual

Self-reflection

1. In what situations do you need to be more open? What actions will you take?
2. In what situations do you need to establish clearer boundaries with certain people? What actions will you take?

OPTIMISM

Too Much————————versus————————Too Little

Where do you generally fall on this spectrum?

Leaders see opportunities where others see problems. They have hope when others have despair.

Too much optimism! Everything will be great. We don't need a backup plan.

Do you ever look at things through rose-colored glasses? Exaggerated optimism can cause you to ignore the warning signs of trouble.

Overly optimistic leaders often have the attitude that everything will be easy. In truth, change is hard work! Some things look easy until you try to do them. In addition, it's very challenging to keep performing at a high-energy level.

Too little optimism! Our presentation probably won't be that good.

Blah, blah, blah! Some leaders project very little optimism for their mission and ideas. People think—*If my leader isn't excited about her mission and vision, then why should I care?*

Leaders who focus all their attention and comments on the obstacles and things that can go wrong drain the energy out of the room.

Doom and gloom!

You can't influence and inspire people with negativity.

Having the right amount of optimism means you're realistic and you see possibilities others may not see.

Read on to find out how others have found their sweet spot.

What's your approach? Comments from the field.

"Think of passion as energy, drive, direction, and focus. Is it possible to have too much? In my experience, the answer is yes. Passion says you care. Too much passion suggests you're out of touch.

Too much passion makes you:

► Speak first, loudest, and longest. You overwhelm people.

► Close your mind; you're too certain.

► Aim too high in the short-term.

► Minimize problems and overestimate abilities.

► Not see and understand the strengths and weaknesses of others."

---Dan Rockwell, Leadership Coach and Author of the Leadership Freak blog

"Sometimes you have to operate with extreme optimism. I was working at Travelers in Hartford, CT, running the servicing units that supported the individual life and disability businesses. The competitive landscape was rapidly changing and our product portfolio was slow to respond. As a result, achieving the financial plan was in jeopardy. Reducing expenses was the only lever we could pull. The CEO suggested relocating the servicing operations to an alternative location in an effort to reduce expenses by 30%.

As I analyzed the location option, I decided to analyze our workflow and supporting systems. I wanted to retain our Connecticut staff.

I had no idea if we could optimize the workflow to achieve the expense-reduction target. Here's where my extreme optimism was needed. I met with my group and told them what the deal was. I exhibited total optimism and confidence in them. I told them they had the knowledge and creativity to redesign the workflow to align with the cost model. Even though I was full of doubt, I told them it was "our moment" and we had the opportunity to control the outcome. Unwavering optimism was needed to make them believe they could design a workflow option that would outperform the alternative location plan."

---Mary Jean Thornton, former Senior Executive at The Travelers, and Professor of Business Administration

"In a leadership role, I find your first passion has to be your people. When I find myself losing passion for my people, it's usually because I'm going after something I want or some arbitrary goal that has been set for me. Maintain your passion for and invest in your people, and you'll find both success and satisfaction."

---Stephanie Angel, Executive Editor at the Lansing State Journal

Self-reflection

1. In what situations do you need to exhibit more optimism?
2. In what situations do you need to be more realistic about what's possible?

PROVIDING INFORMATION

Too Much————versus————Too Little

Do you ever give people too much or too little information?

The best leaders provide the right amount of information at the right time. They communicate what is useful and relevant.

Don't overwhelm people with data dumps.

Effective leaders simplify the complex. And, they use the appropriate communication channel (texting, e-mail, phone, face-to-face, video, etc.) to convey their message.

Too much information! I have 128 slides to explain our team's mission.

Information overload is common these days. When leaders over-communicate, people get overwhelmed and feel confused. Not good!

We want leaders who clarify, simplify, and inspire us to move forward.

Too little information! I have nothing to say.

People want to understand the big picture and have the information they need to effectively do their jobs.

Do you ever withhold information that could benefit your employees? When people don't get the information they need, they are hindered to perform at their best.

Determining what information to share starts by thinking about your audience. What do they need to know? What will engage, focus, and motivate them?

Read on to find out how others have found their sweet spot.

What's your approach? Comments from the field.

"There is an old saying— 'Information is power.' Well, sharing information gives power to the people in your group.

I try to share the appropriate information with each team member that will help them be thoughtful and creative in doing their assigned tasks. The right info can motivate team members to excel.

During times of emotional upheaval, I think it's important to reduce the tension, clarify the task, and set clear priorities.

Each person is unique. It's important to communicate the right information that addresses their needs and wants."

---Kate Bolduc, Director, Strategic Partnerships, Goodwin College. Former Executive at Travelers and CEO of the Hartford Arts Council

"I try to communicate only one central idea or request per email. If I have three different issues, I send three e-mails."

---Judy Zaiken, Corporate Vice President, LL Global, Inc.

Self-reflection

1. In what situations do you need to provide more relevant information so people know what's happening? What actions will you take?
2. In what situations do you provide too much information?

RULES AND POLICIES

Too Much————versus————Too Few

How many rules are necessary?

Some rules and policies are needed. Simple, clear rules and policies work best. Highly regulated industries, like banking and aerospace, have many rules and requirements they must follow.

Effective leaders implement the appropriate number of rules to create both an effective and efficient operation.

Too many rules! We need a policy regarding the number of bathroom breaks allowed per shift.

Bureaucratic organizations have rules for everything. Excess rules often target problem employees at the expense of the many proficient employees.

For rules to be meaningful, they must be enforced; that requires both people and time, which may not be the most effective use of those resources.

Having too many rules sucks the energy and enthusiasm out of an organization. People feel less empowered. This is never a good thing!

Too few rules! We have no rules regarding quality and safety.

On the other hand, too few rules create chaos and a very inefficient operation.

You need the right number of rules to create order, but not so many that people feel like they are in a straitjacket.

Author Jim Collins suggests that if you hire the right people, they don't need a lot of rules. The right people are disciplined and know what to do.

Periodically review your rules and policies to make sure they are appropriate to support an orderly and efficient operation.

Read on to find out how others have found their sweet spot.

What's your approach? Comments from the field.

"Rules – finding the sweet spot is an ongoing process. I also call rules—policies and standards that elicit specific desired behaviors. Too many rules and policies create an inefficient bureaucracy. At the other extreme, too few rules and policies lead to confusion and wasted time.

Organizations need the right number of rules to achieve optimal performance. If performance is below what's required, it may signal there are too many or too few rules or policies, or it may indicate the rules and policies aren't enforced.

Leaders need to define and closely monitor key performance metrics and ensure the appropriate rules, policies, and standards are in place to support how people behave and what they achieve.

Leaders need to model the desired behaviors and hold people accountable to what's expected."

---Karen Martin, President TKMG Inc, (Author and Consultant)

"What's the reason for the rule? Is the rule in place to help produce a more efficient operation, or is it in place because of the performance (or lack thereof) of one or a few individuals? Creating a new rule for everybody, when you are just trying to modify the behavior of a few people, isn't a good practice.

We've never come up with a good guideline for the number of rules that are required, but I'm generally a fan of the concept of less is better. It's certainly easier to remember a few rules. Senior leaders can create more impact by constantly reinforcing a few rules rather than a long list of rules that they will likely forget as well."

---Michael Vann, Senior Consultant, The Vann Group, LLC

Self-reflection

1. What rules/policies need to be changed or deleted?
2. What new rule or policy is needed to improve efficiency?

SUPPLYING FEEDBACK

Too Much————versus————Too Little

How much and how often do you provide feedback on people's performance?

People need constructive feedback to improve.

Top leaders provide people with just the right amount of feedback at the right time. Their feedback is specific, timely, and helpful.

Too much feedback! Here are 28 things you need to improve on!

Most people are open to feedback that identifies one or two changes they need to make to be more effective.

I once observed a high school freshman football coach interacting with his players during a game. He made 41 negative comments and 2 positive comments. After the game, I asked a player if he thought the coach was effective. He said, "Everyone hates the coach, all he does is yell at you and tell you how bad you are." Obviously, that's not effective feedback.

Feedback that is too general or vague isn't helpful.

An important lesson I learned is that feedback delivered with anger is ineffective. People focus on the anger and not what they need to do to improve.

Too little feedback! I never know how I am doing.

Some leaders provide little or no feedback. People aren't sure if their performance is exceptional, mediocre, or poor.

High performers want frequent feedback. They want to know what needs attention and how they can improve.

Leaders who are motivated by their desire to be liked resist giving negative feedback. That's not good.

The right type and amount of feedback delivered at the right time helps people improve their skills and performance. Keep it simple, and focus on one or two things at a time. Also, set the example - ask your employees for suggestions on what you can do to be a better leader.

Read on to find out how others have found their sweet spot.

What's your approach? Comments from the field.

"Balanced feedback is needed. After a game, each player is required to review a video of the game and identify one thing he did well and one thing he could improve. This form of delegation empowers the player to know his strengths and identify one thing he needs to work on.

There is a fine line between giving a player too much or too little feedback, and equally important is keeping it simple. A simple message is more likely to get through. I try not to complicate any of the interactions I have with players."

> ---*Robert Emery, Varsity Hockey Coach,*
> *Plattsburgh State University*

"One of the biggest detractors to giving feedback is the leader's fear in having a difficult conversation. Many times, they say nothing. Their silence condones the employee's behavior and leaves the employee thinking he or she is doing a good job. The problem doesn't go away; it grows. It drives the leader to the point of not being able to hold back any longer. They explode which is not helpful, nor does it resolve the situation.

Constructive feedback is given on a regular basis. And it's best to frame the feedback as it relates to the employee's long-term goals and career desires. When you do this, you show the employees that you care about them and want to help them achieve their desired level of success by highlighting areas of growth for them.

Then, there is the other extreme where the leader micro-manages the employee staying on top of their every move. When this happens, the employee feels like they can do nothing right. They shut down and ultimately look for another job."

---Belinda Pruyne, CEO, Business Innovations Group

"If someone does something great or someone does something poorly, tell them immediately. If it's good news, it's great to provide the positive feedback publicly. If it's bad news, always, always, ALWAYS do it in private. But that's for immediate good and bad items. What I've found as a leader is that most feedback opportunities don't necessarily fit neatly into one of those two buckets, and typically are designed more for long-term performance discussions. I'll break this one into 'timing' and 'content.'

When it comes to 'timing,' how often should you be providing feedback to your employees? The general rule of thumb is that if your employees are only finding out about their performance at year-end, that's not good leadership. Conversely, regardless of what your younger employees might be looking for, daily feedback is probably too much. What's the sweet spot? Honestly, it depends. I've been trending towards having scheduled one-on-ones at least once a month for experienced employees, twice a month for inexperienced employees, and sometimes as often as weekly for struggling employees (regardless of experience level).

On the 'content' side, this will absolutely vary, but regardless I try to let them talk first. Sometimes it's as simple as 'What's on your mind?' and sometimes I ask them something like 'You've been working on XYZ these past couple of weeks. How do you think you've been doing on it?' When I give feedback, I leverage a style I learned in Toastmasters, which is the 'Here's what you did well, and here's what I'd like to see you try differently next time.' Last, but certainly not least, feedback needs to go both ways. I almost always end the one-on-one discussions with asking them what they think I could do better to help them specifically or the team in general."

---Robert J. Parslow, CPA, CMA, Senior Director at a Fortune 100 Healthcare Company

Self-reflection

1. In what situations would more precise feedback be beneficial?
2. Does the feedback you give maintain the person's self-esteem?
3. In what situations are you providing too much feedback?

SUMMARY—FINDING THE RIGHT SPOT

To move from being a good leader to a great leader, you need to find the right spot—your leadership sweet spot in each situation.

Realize that when it comes to coaching, discussing, collaborating, delegating, providing feedback, etc., there is a fine line between doing too much and too little of each leadership behavior.

Each situation is unique and may require you to alter or tweak your approach. As things change, you also need to adjust what you do to make the most positive impact. Keep an open mind. Generally, once we label a person or situation, we put on blinders to all evidence that contradicts our diagnosis.

The best leaders are able to diagnose situations and determine what words and actions will produce the most positive impact. Create a checklist that will help you diagnose the unique aspects of each situation.

Let's be real. You, me, and every other leader makes mistakes. There are times when what you say or do has little or no positive results and may even make things worse.

The best leaders learn from their mistakes. They adjust their approach and become more effective over time.

It's a journey! Every day there are new insights to be considered.

Be open and curious. Identify small opportunities to pilot ideas and learn what you're thinking and doing when you are the most effective.

There is always room to improve and operate more consistently in your *leadership sweet spot*.

Paul B. Thornton

PART II

FINDING THE RIGHT RATIO

Baseball players must be able to catch and throw the ball—two related activities. Of course, how frequently they catch and throw depends on the flow of the game. In a similar way, leaders also engage in related activities, such as:

- ▶ Talking and Listening
- ▶ Managing and Leading
- ▶ Planning and Implementing

In these situations, finding your sweet spot involves finding the right balance or ratio between two related activities.

Consider some of the recent situations you were in. How much time did you spend talking, and how much did you spend listening? Did you have the right balance? Could a different ratio have made you more effective?

Manager and Leader

One of the big-ticket items that you must get right is the amount of time you spend managing and leading.

There is a significant difference in each role!

- ▶ **Managers** use current methods, procedures, and resources to get the job done. Managers want stability. They want to maintain the status quo.
- ▶ **Leaders** use their words and actions to influence and inspire others to make positive changes. Leaders want change. They want to improve the status quo.

Some leaders overmanage and under-lead. What does that mean? Too much stability and not enough change. They don't change fast enough to keep up with the demanding, dynamic marketplace. That doesn't help the organization stay relevant or competitive.

On the other hand, some leaders over-lead and under-manage. What does that mean? Too much change and not enough stability. These leaders try to change too much, too fast. Too much change results in chaos and confusion. Employees get exhausted and stressed out, which produces an ineffective and inefficient operation.

You need to manage and lead but do it in the right ratio. Of course, the right amount of time you spend doing each role depends on your position in the organization and the amount of change going on in your industry.

The topics in this section require you to think about the amount of time you spend doing two related activities.

The big questions for you to consider are:

1. Do you have the right balance in each area?
2. Would a change in your ratio make you a more effective leader?

ACTION AND REFLECTION

What's your ratio between taking action and reflecting on what was done?

- **Take action**. This refers to what you say and do.
- **Reflection**. This refers to thinking about your assumptions, actions, and the results that were achieved.

Leaders are action-oriented. They do the following:

- Speak up for their core beliefs and values
- Make presentations to inspire people to pursue bigger goals and ideals
- Conduct experiments and pilot programs to discover better ways of doing things.

Leaders implement change. But they also need to take time to reflect on what's being done, why it's being done, and the effectiveness of the results. They question and analyze their assumptions and the approach they used in various situations. They also consider the big picture—where they are going and what they can become.

Leaders use a variety of methods to reflect, including keeping a diary, spending time alone to think, and discussing their insights with mentors and friends. Some leaders use specific questions to guide their thinking:

- Where were the gaps between what I thought would happen and what actually happened?
- What worked well today?
- What changes are needed?

Author and coach John Maxwell (Founder of the John Maxwell Team) acknowledges that reflection turns experience into insight.

If you are in a constant state of go, go, go—do, do, do, you never take time to think and learn. This is not good. It's important to step back from the fray and ponder what's working and what's not working.

Some balance between action and reflection is needed. What's the right balance? Of course, it depends on the situation but some reflection is required to grow and develop.

How much time do you spend reflecting?

Read on to find out how others have found the appropriate balance between *taking action* and *reflection.*

What's your approach? Comments from the field.

"My ratio is 60/40. Sixty percent on reflect. That's a lot, but taking time to reflect is very critical. If you don't reflect and learn, you keep making the same mistakes.

Some of the things I do to reflect include simply thinking about what happened, keeping a journal, discussing situations with my mentor or boss.

Group reflection is also useful. After a major team event, it's important to have a team debrief. But before that, I think each individual needs a day or two to do some personal reflection. Team debriefs are more likely to work if you establish rules of engagement such as be open, offer specific suggestions for improvement, no personal attacks, etc. If you're the leader, go first and indicate what you could have done better. Set a positive example."

---Kate Labor, Vice President of Sales, System and Software

"Solitude to quiet your mind, self-reflect, rest, and plan your future is the difference between focused and frantic.

Always 'on' is a destructive myth.

No one gives 100% effort 100% of the time."

---Dan Rockwell, Leadership Coach and Author of the Leadership Freak blog

"What's the right balance? I'm a big believer in reflection. Without it, you keep making the same mistakes.

Action and reflection is a back-and-forth process. Take some small actions, create energy and momentum, then reflect. Tweak your plan. Learn as you go.

Reflection can take 5 minutes or 50 minutes. I like to get my whole team involved in the reflection step. Get multiple points of view, and everybody learns.

It's also important I take time to work on myself. Reflect on what I do or don't do as a leader. I have a couple of colleagues who give me valuable feedback."

---Frank Deane, CEO, Lumleian LLC

Self-reflection

1. In what situations do you need to be more action-oriented?
2. In what situations would more reflection be helpful? What actions will you take?

BIG CHANGES AND SMALL CHANGES

Does your organization, department, or team need a tweak or a major overhaul?

- ▶ **Big changes** refer to major changes such as changing the mission or culture, adding a new product line, implementing new technologies, and making acquisitions.

- ▶ **Small changes** refer to daily opportunities to make minor changes to improve results. Think about this as continuous improvement.

There are times when big changes are needed, and there are always opportunities to make small improvements.

Some leaders try to pursue too many big change initiatives at the same time. The problem is that you don't have the time and resources to make 13 major changes all at once. In addition, people can't handle the demands and stress that this creates.

It's best to focus on one big change at a time! You need to explain "why" big change is needed in a compelling and inspiring way. Employees need to embrace what they are being asked to do.

Every company has small problems that create inefficiencies. They slow things down, cause confusion, and frustrate employees and customers. Several of these problems can be worked on simultaneously.

In addition, there are always opportunities to improve some of your soft skills, such as communicating, listening, resolving conflicts, and providing feedback.

It's best to focus on a few, maybe 3-to-5, small changes at a time. Continuous improvement needs to be a daily focus.

I think pursuing one or two major changes and a few small changes is the best ratio for most leaders.

Read on to find out how others have found the appropriate balance between pursuing *big changes* and *small changes*.

What's your approach? Comments from the field.

"Today's reality is constant change. When multiple changes are happening at the same time, it impacts employee engagement and morale. It's stressful. Priorities need to be reset on a daily basis. It's challenging.

Sure, it would be better to have more balance here, focus on one or two big changes at a time. But with acquisitions, workflow changes, state and federal regulations changes, new technology, etc. there is a lot hitting you all at once."

---Neil Altieri, Director, New Business and Underwriting, MassMutual

"Leaders can face some big challenges—I did! A major funder substantially cut their support. The first thing I had to do was, face reality, face the facts. It was a critical time for me and the organization. It's important to look at the opportunities in front of you. There are solutions to every problem if you have the right mindset. Broaden your mindset. The worst thing you can do is narrow your thinking and hope things will change.

It's also important to continue making small improvement. It comes down to having good habits; our habits drive what we do day-to-day."

---Dr. Rebecca Corbin, President and CEO, NACCE (National Association for Community College Entrepreneurship)

Self-reflection

1. What big changes are needed to leapfrog the competition?
2. What small changes will improve your overall operation? What actions will you take?
3. What changes will improve your effectiveness as a leader?

BIG PICTURE AND KEY DETAILS

How much time do you spend focusing on the big picture versus important details?

- ▸ **Big Picture** refers to the major economic, political, social, and technological factors that influence customers, employees, and businesses.
- ▸ **Key Details** refers to minor but important factors that relate to plans, proposals, processes, and achieving success.

Do you remember the zoom button on your camera? Zoom out and see the *big picture;* zoom in and get a close-up of *the details.*

Big picture thinkers are often the visionaries who have lots of exciting ideas. These leaders are comfortable operating at the macro level. They are fully aware of the major forces impacting their environment and business.

Can you see the forest from the trees?

Detail-oriented people are more practical and hands-on. They are good at identifying the small but important details and actions needed to successfully implement change.

Some leaders spend all their time putting out fires; they get in the weeds and stay there. I know one leader who is obsessed with his to-do list but lacks a big picture to guide him. This is not a good way to lead!

There are times when it's most important to step back and see the big picture to understand the major forces driving change. There are other times when you need to dig into the details and get a close-up view of how things are operating.

What's the right ratio? It depends on many factors including your industry, the competition, and the specific performance problems in your organization.

Read on to find out how others have found the appropriate balance between focusing on the big picture and key details.

What's your approach? Comments from the field.

"It pays to look at opportunity with a telescope-- it's real, but it's distant. The telescope brings it into focus and helps you find your way there. Telescopes are easy to find if you look for them.

And it often pays to look at trouble with a microscope. Not to get intimidated by the amorphous blob that could snuff out your dreams, but instead to look at the tiny component parts, learning how it is constructed and taking away its power. Once you realize how it's built, you can deal with it."

---Seth Godin, Author, Blogger and Entrepreneur

"I spend 60 percent of my time on the big picture. I try to focus my time and attention on the major customer issues, what the competition is doing, how well we are competing in the marketplace, and our overall company strategy. If things aren't going well in our business, I get pulled into the details. That's something to avoid—don't get pulled into the weeds.

One detail that I track is getting the pulse of our top 10 performers. What are they thinking and feeling? That's important info."

---Kate Labor, Vice President of Sales, System and Software

"Don't sweat the small stuff.' While there is some truth in that statement, it's important to remember lasting change always starts with the small things.

Little hinges swing big doors. Habits and discipline are both behaviors that have a massive impact on our lives. They are seemingly small things, yet they have an out-sized impact on our success.

So, it's important to sweat the *right* small stuff, and realize it isn't so little after all."

---Kevin Eikenberry, Founder, The Kevin Eikenberry Group (Author, Speaker, and Consultant)

"What is the right balance of focusing on the big picture and details? This is like asking whether my right leg is more important than my left leg. I need both to be able to walk properly. Likewise, today's dynamic business environment requires leaders to span both horizons –the big picture and the finer details simultaneously. Leaders today don't have the luxury of choosing between the two. External stakeholders, as well as your own teams, will not respect you unless you have a firm grasp of both – the big picture and the minutiae.

Should a leader be spending 50% of his time in each area? Life does not neatly add to 100%. So, one needs to show 100% attention to the big picture and 100% attention to the details."

> ---*Rostow Ravanan, CEO & MD, Mindtree*

Self-reflection

1. What is one specific action could you take to better understand the big picture?
2. What details should you pay more attention to?

CARROTS AND STICKS

What's your ratio of using carrots and sticks to motivate your people?

▶ **Carrots** refer to all things that are used to reward and recognize positive performance. Praise, pay raises, promotions, time off, and team celebrations make people feel good about themselves and their accomplishments.

▶ **Sticks** refer to negative things such as verbal and written warnings, negative feedback, and demotions that are used to get people's attention and motivate them to change.

Top leaders realize not all carrots and sticks have the same effect on people. Some people relish public praise, while others hate it. Learn what carrots and sticks have the most positive impact on each of your team members.

A few years ago, I attended the Gino Auriemma UCONN Leadership Conference. He is the highly successful women's basketball coach (11 national championships) at the University of Connecticut. After observing one of his practices, it became clear to me that Auriemma is highly skilled at figuring out what carrots and sticks to use to motivate each player.

Some leaders only operate on the positive side, always ready to dole out praise and recognition, but they never administer the "sticks."

High performing people get annoyed when poor performance is not addressed.

At the other extreme, some leaders only use sticks. They are quick to criticize and discipline, but never praise and highlight accomplishments. They only focus on the negatives. These leaders think people are unaspiring and careless—not good!

Jack Welch got it right when he said, "...good leaders know when to hug and when to kick." Both are necessary. Each one has a time and place, but the challenge is knowing when to do which.

What's the right ratio? The situation determines what's required.

Most of the time you will use more carrots than sticks but remember "sticks" is a form of tough love. Taking disciplinary action shows you really care about people and want them to change and improve.

Read on to find out how others have found the appropriate balance between using *carrots* and *sticks* to motivate people.

What's your approach? Comments from the field.

"As leaders, we need both carrot and stick, but it's best to rely on the stick as little as possible.

The team has to know that the stick is there, and they have to believe that you are willing to use it if warranted. The problem with the stick is that we can only threaten, prod, or punish. And when someone shakes a stick at us, our focus becomes avoiding the stick, not on performing to our capacity.

For top performance, the carrot is the far better tool. With well-chosen ones, we can orient people on a goal and encourage them to pursue it. Given the right carrot, people focus on *doing* **instead of** *avoiding* and will reach beyond themselves to give their very best. The more time we spend looking for what is going right and handing out carrots, the less time we end up worrying about the stick. Best of all, some of the most powerful carrots, like praise, are free."

---Ken Downer, author of the Rapid Start Leadership blog

"Over the course of my career, I have found that this is more a question of context and personal philosophy. For example, in the context of a prison, a stick approach is more relevant; whereas in an ad agency, a carrot approach is more appropriate. One style does not fit all situations. Also, some leaders find one approach more natural, so they stick to it and that's perfectly fine. If I talk of myself personally, I use both methods, depending on the situation."

---Rostow Ravanan, CEO & MD, Mindtree

"One of the most useful 'carrots' I've found is just saying 'thank you' for jobs that are even slightly above and beyond normal performance. If someone put in a lot of effort to get something done, praise that effort.

If your company allows for other forms of recognition, leverage that as best you can, but make sure you understand what's really a 'carrot' for that person. For example, sending someone to a conference might be a 'carrot' for one employee and a total pain for a different employee. I've done everything from providing extra days off to sending gift cards to restaurants I know they like.

Figure out what works and what's feasible, but never ever forget to say, 'thank you' when someone goes above and beyond."

---Robert J. Parslow, CPA, CMA, Senior Director at a Fortune 100 Healthcare Company

Self-reflection

1. In what situations do you need to use more carrots?
2. In what situations do you need to use a stick to change behavior?

DISCOVERY AND DELIVERY

What is your ratio of time spent discovering new products, and time spent working to improve the delivery of your products?

- ► **Discovery** refers to the actions taken to identify new products and services that customers will want to buy.
- ► **Delivery** refers to the actions taken to deliver products and services in the most efficient way.

Ron Shaich, CEO of Panera Bread, believes there are two essential requirements of operating any successful business: discovery and delivery. Every few months, Panera Bread demonstrates discovery by announcing the addition of a few new items on their menu.

In addition, they periodically demonstrate delivery by implementing a new process that makes it easier to place and/or pick up an order.

Each action, discovery and delivery, requires a different focus and set of skills. The discovery process requires collaborating and brainstorming to come up with new products and services.

The delivery process involves flowcharting, measuring, analyzing, and simplifying processes and procedures to improve efficiency.

If you focus too much on discovery and underemphasize delivery, you create great products that are poorly delivered.

On the other hand, if you spend all your time focusing on delivery, you may end up producing the same old products and services that customers no longer want.

You need to find the right balance between discovery and delivery so your company continues to grow and consistently meets customer expectations.

Read on to find out how others have found the appropriate balance between *discovery* and *delivery*.

What's your approach? Comments from the field.

"Achieving the appropriate balance between discovery and delivery is very important. Leaders need to consider a variety of factors, including customers' wants and needs and what they complain about. Also, consider what the competition is doing and the overall rate of change in the market.

- ▶ **Discovery**—this is one approach. Try it and see what works. Fail fast—use that failure to learn and improve. Some companies are fortunate to have big R & D budgets. Some companies compensate executives for achieving revenue targets that are generated from new products.
- ▶ **Delivery** can often be improved by removing clutter. Simplify. Prune what no longer adds value.

Here's the balance I recommend: On a regular basis, try to identify one or two new great products or services. Couple that with flawless delivery, that's a winning formula.

If you don't keep reinventing and improving your products, services, and yourself, you start to fall behind the competition."

---Jim Clemmer, President, The Clemmer Group

"I put the customer at the center of both discovery and delivery—it's critical to know your customer. Who is your target market? What are their needs and wants? Simple questions—but not always answered with precision.

One thing I learned, that challenged my assumptions, was a lot of my customers were buying my scarves and ponchos to hide things they didn't like about their appearance rather than as a fashion statement. It hadn't occurred to me that hiding things was a major motivation. The more I know about my customers, the better I am at making needed changes to my products and services.

I do a lot of face-to-face selling, so "delivery" is more about the shopping experience for the customer. If the experience doesn't meet or exceed what the customer expects, I've lost a customer."

---Diane Sabato, Professor of Business Administration and Small Business Owner

Self-Reflection

1. Are you spending the right amount of time trying to identify new products and services? What actions do you need to take?

2. Are you spending the right amount of time to improve the delivery of your products and services? What actions are required?

EFFECTIVE AND EFFICIENT

Do you concentrate more on being effective or efficient?

▶ **Effective** refers to being focused on the right things. Effective leaders are focused on the right problems and opportunities. They have the right goals and priorities.

▶ **Efficient** refers to using your resources in the most productive way-- no waste. Waste produces unnecessary costs.

Some leaders use all their resources in the most productive ways, but they are focused on the wrong things. This is not good!

One of the biggest wastes of time is being efficient at doing something that doesn't need to be done. Some people are highly efficient at creating beautiful spreadsheets with a wealth of data that no one wants or needs.

It's easy to lose focus because the marketplace is dynamic and fast-changing. In today's business environment, you must be *agile*—able to make quick changes and a total pivot if needed.

Are you consistently focused on the right things?

At the other extreme, some leaders are focused on the right things, but they are wasteful in how they use their resources.

Today, profit margins are being squeezed, and the competition keeps improving. You need to have a *lean* operation—no fat, no waste. Efficient processes are required in every business.

High performing leaders are both effective and efficient.

What can you do?

Constantly assess the changing landscape and make sure you are focused on the right things. It starts with being effective. If you are ineffective, you are wasting your time.

Periodically, evaluate how you are using each of your resources and make sure you are maximizing efficiency. Frequently, ask yourself if what you're doing at any given moment needs to be done.

Read on to find out how others have found the appropriate balance to be both *effective* and *efficient*.

What's your approach? Comments from the field.

"I lead a group of 35 people (5 physician assistants and 30 office staff). Having both an efficient and effective operation is critical.

For me, 'efficiency' means having clearly defined goals and getting things done without errors. Mistakes create rework, which wastes time. I also try to be an efficient communicator—succinct—get to the bottom-line point quickly, but use words and terms that will be understood by the receiver.

To be 'effective,' I always do a proper diagnosis of the patient's situation to ensure I am addressing the true problem-- getting the patient's history is key.

I have learned that to be both effective and efficient it helps to anticipate issues and problems that might occur. When you anticipate what might happen, you're better prepared."

---Gino Mercadante, MD. Director of the Ludlow Medical Center

"Effectiveness definitely comes first, but only to a particular point. Here's what I mean:

If the team isn't getting the job done, then focus on effectiveness. But once you get your team to a solid level of performance, what I do is switch the team towards efficiency. What I want to know is: 'How can we get the same answer, but get it faster?'

I'll leverage the efficiency gains to build capacity in the team. Then—and here's the key—use that capacity to increase the team's effectiveness. Make the whole process/product/answer/etc., better...a new level of effectiveness. And then go make it more efficient, and so on."

---Robert J. Parslow, CPA, CMA, Senior Director at a Fortune 100 Healthcare Company

"What assets do we have right now that we're not taking advantage of?"

---Virgil, Latin Poet, Author, and Philosopher

Self-reflection

1. What actions do you take to ensure you are focused on the right things?
2. Are your best people working on the biggest opportunities?
3. What is one action that you could take to be more efficient?

FIRM AND FLEXIBLE

Do you know when to be firm and when to be flexible?

- **Firm** refers to being certain, unwavering, and unchanging.
- **Flexible** refers to being willing to adjust, change, and modify.

Great leaders are firm on their core beliefs, principles, and values. They don't waver on the important stuff. They know where to draw the line.

Being "firm" lets people know what you stand for and what they can expect from you.

Leaders who lack strong convictions come across as indecisive and wishy-washy.

However, there are times when you need to be flexible. Policies, strategies, and tactics need to be adjusted as conditions change. When you collaborate and negotiate, you need to be flexible and willing to modify your position.

Some leaders refuse to change, even when all the data indicates it's a flawed strategy! Being close-minded and rigid when you should be open and flexible can be a fatal flaw.

Can you be too flexible? Yes!

Some leaders change with the wind. Their current position is based on the last person they spoke with. These leaders lose credibility very quickly.

Can your employees predict when you will be unwavering and firm?

Read on to find out how others have determined when to be *firm* and when to be *flexible*.

What's your approach? Comments from the field.

"You need to be both firm and flexible. The key is to know where and when to apply one or the other.

To be the leader that others look up to and ultimately choose to follow, you must stand firm on your core beliefs/values. I call these your *core non-negotiable values*, the things you draw the line in the cement for, not the sand. They become what you are known for, allow you to lead from a clear vision, and tell others why you are the right leader for the job.

If you don't know what your core non-negotiable values are or compromise on them all the time, then you won't be able to lead. Your lack of consistency will confuse others, chisel away at your confidence, and lessen your credibility with others.

Get clear on what matters most to you, your *core non-negotiable values,* and stand firm. Guide others from this place of clarity and become the leader that others follow!"

---Belinda Pruyne, CEO, Business Innovations Group

"In matters of style, swim with the current; in matters of principle, stand like a rock."

---*Thomas Jefferson*
Founding Father and former US President

"It's easy to be firm – just quote the rule or policy. But that negatively impacts morale and productivity.

I lean towards being flexible. I work with bright, talented people who are highly motivated. They don't need a lot of rules and regulations.

But there are times when I am 100% firm. There is no room for debate when it comes to ethics or doing something that will hurt the company's reputation.

On occasion, but it's rare, I am firm on the steps or actions people must take to meet customer expectations."

---*Frank Deane, CEO, Lumleian LLC*

Self-Reflection

1. Are you crystal clear and firm on your core beliefs and values?

2. In what situations do you need to be more firm? What actions will you take?

3. In what situations do you need to show more flexibility? What actions will you take?

FORMAL STRUCTURE AND INFORMAL NETWORK

Do you fully utilize the formal and informal structure to achieve your goals?

- ▶ **Formal Structure** is represented by the organizational chart. It indicates who reports to whom, chain of command, levels of management, and span of control.

- ▶ **Informal Network** refers to the social, informal interactions that occur between people. It can be diagrammed by drawing lines that represent all the conversations that occur within the organization.

The formal structure identifies the formal communication channel, who has position power, and the pecking order to escalate issues and resolve problems.

In the formal structure, it's important to build relationships with the people who have the positional power; they make decisions and assign resources.

The informal network provides insights into the following:

- ▶ Who talks with whom to get work done
- ▶ Who socializes with whom
- ▶ Who people go to for guidance
- ▶ How information flows through the grapevine

The informal network identifies the influential members of the group. These members set the tone for the group, serve as a sounding board for new ideas, and influence the acceptance of change initiatives. The informal network tells you how people are feeling about their job, co-workers, and the company.

The informal network identifies the informal leaders who you need to win over to support your ideas.

Some leaders just focus on the formal structure. They think that just moving the boxes on the org chart or shuffling people into new boxes will significantly improve performance. It seldom does.

The informal networks need to support the company's mission, vision, and strategy.

How much time do you invest in working the formal structure and informal network? Is your ratio appropriate?

Read on to find out how others have found the appropriate balance between utilizing the *formal structure* and *informal networks* to achieve their goals.

What's your approach? Comments from the field.

"Too much structure: Organizations have the tendency to 'stiffen in' over time. More rules, more bureaucracy, rigid structures are weakening the organization's vitality and slowing decisions down. Informal networks can be useful to get direct access to decision makers, to enhance necessary decisions, or to simply get things done. The organization naturally balances the rigidity by adding informal agility."

---Julia Culen, Executive Coach and Management Consultant

"Altering the organization's structure might be necessary but approaching change by changing the organization chart alone is insufficient in most cases. Over the years, a pseudo-science has emerged that focuses on finding the perfect organization chart— we call this boxology. Even if a perfect organization chart did exist (with the right spans of control, optimal layers of management, proper placement of talent, clear decision rights, etc.), structure is just one aspect of organization design.

Organizations are complex systems, with changes in one area cascading and sometimes setting off changes throughout the entire system. Moreover, organizations operate in complex environments with market forces, competitors' behaviors, and regulatory requirements demanding that an organization continually change and adapt.

One risk of boxology is that it ignores the interdependency of organizational components like work, culture, structure, metrics, rewards, etc. It ignores the deep connections of those components to forces at play in the organization's environment. It also ignores the reality of how work is done, who makes decisions, and how resources are allocated. Truly effective organization design is about finding the optimal alignment of all of these components—not simply trying to optimize the structure of the organization. Indeed, structure only enables or disables strategy. In and of itself, structure doesn't create or deliver value to the customer."

**---Ken Brophy, Consultant, AlignOrg
Solutions**

(The term "boxology" is from <u>Mastering the Cube: Overcoming Stumbling blocks and Building Organizations that Work</u>, *by Reed Deshler, Kreig Smith, and Alyson Von Feldt).*

Self-reflection

1. What actions could you take to more effectively utilize the formal structure?
2. What relationships do you need to strengthen in the informal network?

HARD DATA AND SOFT DATA

Do you consider both the hard data and soft data when analyzing situations and making decisions?

- ▶ **Hard Data** refers to the numbers and facts—statements that are concrete and provable.
- ▶ **Soft Data** refers to people's feelings, emotions, and confidence--how people feel about the present situation and the future.

Every February, the National Football League runs a camp called the Scouting Combine. It's done to assess a number of skills of college players. With great precision, the players are evaluated on numerous tests, including the 40-yard dash, bench presses, and vertical leaps.

The scouts collect a lot of hard data. But what about the soft data—the intangibles like confidence, optimism, and leadership that can greatly influence performance on game day?

Effective leaders know that both the hard data and soft data are needed to fully understand any situation.

Certainly, the numbers provide important information about what's happening, but the numbers don't always explain *why* things are happening or how people feel about the hard data.

Some leaders only focus on the financial numbers. With these leaders, if you bring up any touchy-feely stuff, you'll get bounced out of the room.

On the other hand, some leaders lack a full understanding of the numbers and go with their gut-feel. They overemphasize the emotional side of the equation—this is not good!

You also need to use both the *hard data* and *soft data* to sell your ideas!

The hard data may convince the audience, but appealing to their emotions is what moves them to act. It's the strong words and stories that pull at people's heartstrings. The challenge is presenting the right balance of both intellectual arguments and emotional appeals.

Do you have a good balance between using both the hard and soft data to evaluate situations, make decisions, and sell your ideas?

Read on to find out how others have found the right balance between utilizing both the *hard* and *soft data*.

What's your approach? Comments from the field.

"I once observed a senior leader who was hired to turn around a struggling unit. He followed his instinct and studied the hard data. For weeks, he was only seen or heard from when he had questions about various reports or processes. While he was examining the data, employee morale continued to decline. A few key members defected to different departments, and the performance indicators tracked to new lows.

Numbers are important but it's also critical to understand the mindset of the people. What are their concerns and fears? Every person in your newly inherited group is thinking the same thing: 'What do these changes mean for me?' They're in defend mode, at a time you need them to be open and engaged in the change process.

I meet with each person and ask three questions:

▶ What's working?

▶ What's not?

▶ What do you need me to do to help you succeed?

I roll up the key themes I hear during these sessions and share them back with the group for prioritizing and action-plan development. And then I support them as they pursue implementing their improvement ideas."

---Art Petty, Author, Consultant, and Blogger

"I start by looking at the facts. What are the metrics telling me! Next, I consider the question, "Why is this happening?" This is where feelings come into play. If the metrics aren't great, I try to find out why. Does the person or group need training, more staff, or something else?

If the metrics are good or bad, I try to find out how the person or group is feeling about the results. Sometimes when people produce super results, it's because they were working 100 hours a week to get it done. The person may be very pleased with his performance but may feel he can't keep up at this pace.

I find senior leaders overemphasize the facts and metrics. It's all about the numbers, but feelings are an important part of the equation."

---*Kate Bolduc, Director, Strategic Partnerships, Goodwin College. Former Executive at Travelers and CEO of the Hartford Arts Council*

"Big data—the data is out there. You can't be intimidated by the data. You must dissect the data to understand the current environment and use it to make effective decisions.

Feelings also matter, but your gut feelings may be too raw to just go with your gut-feel."

---*Alden Davis, Founder, MyValueTree.com*

Self-reflection

1. In what situations do you need to consider more of the hard data? What actions will you take?
2. In what situations do you need to consider more of the soft data? What actions will you take?

PEOPLE FOCUS AND TASK FOCUS

Do you focus more on the task or your people?

- **Task-Focus** refers to focusing on work that needs to be done.
- **People-Focus** refers to focusing on the people who are doing the work.

It is critical to produce quality products and services that meet and exceed customer expectations.

You must live within budgets and meet deadlines.

But some leaders only focus on the task: *I don't care if you need to work all night or all weekend—get the job done.* These leaders have no concern for the people.

One of my students said that the worst manager she ever had was 100% focused on the task; he never showed any interest or concern for his employees.

The best leaders believe in and take steps to help their people grow, develop, and maximize their contributions. I recommend you spend 80% of your time building on your people's strengths and 20% on areas needing improvement.

Can you overdo the "people-focus"? Yes! Some leaders run their department like a country club; *Is everybody happy and having fun?* They have little concern for getting projects done on time and within budget. That's not good for customers or the business.

Having the appropriate balance between task and people depends on the situation. If an employee is going through a personal crisis, it makes sense to be more focused on him or her than the tasks assigned. When dealing with a major, serious customer issue, all of your attention should be on the problem.

Here's my suggestion—start the day with an evenly balanced focus between the work projects and your people. As events unfold, adjust your focus to address the needs of the day.

Read on to find out how others have found the appropriate balance between being focused on the *task* and *their people*.

What's your approach? Comments from the field.

"My ratio would be 70 percent on the people, and 30 percent on the task.

I try to recruit and hire the right people – the best people. People who will work well together and produce great products.

If you get the right team in place, you don't have to worry about getting the tasks done.

The more time I focus on the people, coaching, and mentoring, the more I'm helping the business grow and develop."

---Frank Deane, CEO, Lumleian LLC

"Obviously both [task-focus, and people-focus] are important and interrelated. You need to adjust your focus to the situation.

An important first step is determining exactly what is the problem:

- Is the task clear?
- Is the goal unrealistic?
- Are people feeling overwhelmed?
- Do people lack needed skills and resources?
- Is there one person who is negatively impacting the team dynamics?

My focus is making sure people have the knowledge, skills, and motivation to succeed in accomplishing the tasks they are assigned."

---Fred Kelly, Area Vice President of Sales, Masimo Corporation

Self-reflection

1. In what situations do you need a stronger focus on the task? What actions will you take?
2. In what situations should you focus more on your people? What actions will you take?

PLANNING AND IMPLEMENTING

Do you spend the appropriate amount of time planning events so implementation will be successful?

- ▶ **Planning** refers to the process used to identify all the resources, actions, and timeline required to achieve the desired goals. It's a logical, linear process.
- ▶ **Implementing** refers to doing what was planned— making it happen. It requires people to start doing the assigned tasks to meet the required due dates.

Having a plan is one thing, but successfully implementing it is something quite different.

At the organizational level, plans are called *strategies*. They describe the approach organizations use to compete and succeed in the marketplace. Creating an effective strategy requires a lot of information and the ability to conceptualize and connect all the dots.

Leaders who are overly action-oriented do little or no planning. Generally, some amount of planning is beneficial.

At the other extreme, some leaders have lengthy planning sessions but think implementation will take care of itself. This doesn't work.

Implementation is the hard part; it requires agility and adaptability. Most implementations don't go as planned, so you need to keep adjusting.

Effective planning requires you to get the right people together to discuss what needs to be done and what resources are needed. Clear roles, responsibilities, and deadlines need to be established.

Planning and implementation go hand-in-hand, but there is no magic formula that tells you how much time you need to spend on planning and implementing.

Here are some factors to consider:

- ▶ In a project with high uncertainty, it may be more applicable to do less planning and be more adaptive and agile as the plan gains clarity.
- ▶ Projects with more certainty allow you to lay out a more precise, detailed plan that may only need tweaking during implementation.

Read on to find out how others have found the right balance between *planning* and *implementation*.

What's your approach? Comments from the field.

"Some leaders think the bulk of their job just involves the planning phase. Create the mission, vision, and strategy and then hand it off to your direct reports for implementation. Sounds good, but it doesn't work.

Leaders need to be actively involved in the implementation. I devoted 50-to-60% of my time to make sure the right things were happening at the right time—not getting in the weeds, but asking questions, probing assumptions, observing first-hand what was being done as well as what wasn't getting done."

---Mary Jean Thornton, a former senior executive at The Travelers and Professor, Business Administration

"A few tactics—3-to-5 is sufficient to support the implementation of most major strategies. Too many tactics create confusion. It's important to delete things that don't work.

These days it's important to be agile and nimble. Simplicity, clear responsibilities, and clear accountabilities are needed."

---Dr. Rebecca Corbin, President, and CEO, NACCE (National Association for Community College Entrepreneurship)

Self-reflection

1. Do you consistently involve the right people in creating the plan?
2. What actions can you take to improve the implementation of your plans?

PRESENT (SHORT TERM) AND FUTURE (LONG TERM)

Do you spend more time focusing on current problems or future opportunities?

▶ **The present** refers to the current week, month, and quarter; it's focusing on the current problems and opportunities.

▶ **The future** refers to the one-to-three-year time-frame; it's focusing on future challenges and opportunities.

Some leaders get overly consumed with present day issues, fighting fires, and doing what's urgent. A colleague described it this way: *"They get so tied up in meetings and hitting the quarterly financials, they don't spend enough time thinking long term."*

Certainly, publicly-traded companies need to be concerned with quarterly earnings, but it's a question of balance. Are you spending 98% of your time on the short term, and 2% on the long term?

Some leaders obsess over the future for several weeks, then they shift their focus and spend 100% of their time on current problems. They swing back and forth between the extremes.

Senior executives who only live in the future don't know the ship is sinking. They're out of touch with day-to-day problems.

Some balance between thinking about the present and the future is needed. Actually, you must be able to think across multiple timeframes—the past, present, and future.

Think about the meetings you attend. How much time is spent discussing the current problems versus future opportunities?

Read on to find out how others have found the right balance between thinking about the *short term* and *the long term*.

What's your approach? Comments from the field.

"Following our ten-year strategic plan, I prioritize my focus and energy based on functional and positioning importance as to which projects should command my immediate attention. Obviously, there are urgent matters that occupy much of my present attention; but, at all times, I have my eye on future directions and continually allocate chunks of time in proportion to desired outcomes and envisioned goals. In the end, it's all about balancing the present with the future, as we learn from the experiences of the past."

---Dr. Nido R. Qubein, President, High Point University

"I focus 80 percent of my time on the future, that being a 1-to-3-year timeframe. I look at political and social trends as well as state and federal laws and regulations. Another important factor is how the workforce is changing. Each generation brings new talents and challenges."

---*Al Kasper, President, Savage Arms*

Self-reflection

1. What trends and opportunities require you to spend more time thinking about the future? What actions will you take?
2. What current problems need more of your attention? What actions will you take?

SYSTEMS AND PROCESSES

How much time do you spend focusing on processes versus the overall system?

- ▶ **Process** refers to the steps taken to produce an output. Some examples of processes include ordering supplies, paying bills, producing parts, and interviewing candidates.
- ▶ **System** refers to how all the processes interact and work together to produce the desired experience and products. It represents the integration of all the parts.

Effective leaders make a point to understand what's happening at both the process level and the system level.

It's important to remember that not all processes are of equal importance. The processes that directly relate to acquiring customers, developing employees, and creating great products and services are most important.

You need to make sure the critical processes are working together in support of the company's strategy and culture.

Systems are complex! Like the human body, there are lots of parts to every business that must be aligned and integrated for the business to perform at the optimal level.

An effective system requires constant monitoring and tweaking to keep all parts working together in the most productive way.

How much time do you spend evaluating how well the overall system is working?

Read on to find out how others have found the appropriate balance between working on various *processes* and the *system*.

What's your approach? Comments from the field.

"General Managers need to value all the key parts of the business and appreciate how the parts fit together and function as a whole.

Some leaders do too much meddling in the function they came from. That's their expertise and comfort level. The problem is the changes they make often negatively impact other parts of the business. This often creates more organizational chaos.

Seasoned executives know that the parts of the overall business model must be properly aligned and integrated, so the whole system works effectively and efficiently. With this knowledge, the executive can selectively choose when and how to intervene to reinforce the urgency of addressing the deficit while minimizing chaos.

You need to keep one eye on the process or workflow, and one eye on the system."

---Mary Jean Thornton, former Senior Executive at The Travelers, and Professor of Business Administration

"Effective leaders are concerned with the system which requires both vertical and horizontal alignment. From the top to the bottom there needs to be clear intentions and goals. The proper cascading of information and resources are needed to make that happen. It's critical to align your day-to-day operations with your overall strategy.

Horizontal alignment is also critical. Work processes, shared decision making and key linkages help insure teams and departments can operate in an integrated way across organizational boundaries.

Alignment is something leaders need to keep working at. It's not a once and done thing. Things are fluid. Change waits for no organization. Leaders need to pay attention, be agile, and keep making changes to stay focused and aligned."

---*Reed Deshler, Managing Director*
AlignOrg Solutions*

Self-Reflection

1. What criteria and metrics do you use to evaluate the overall system?
2. What processes have the biggest impact on the system?
3. Are all parts of your organization aligned in support of the organization's strategy?

TALKING AND LISTENING

What is your talk to listen ratio in most situations?

► **Talking** refers to what is said in both formal and informal settings. It includes making statements and asking questions.

► **Listening** refers to paying attention to the message and ideas that others are conveying. It includes focusing on both what is said and how it is stated, including tone of voice, body language, and energy level.

Top leaders are great communicators. They present their ideas clearly and concisely. They are able to communicate with all the different individuals and groups.

However, some leaders overdue the talking side of the equation. They have big egos and love to talk and talk about all the great things they have accomplished.

Great leaders are curious and eager to learn what others are thinking. They spend significant time listening.

Some leaders start new assignments by going on a "listening tour." They meet with customers, employees, and suppliers to find out what's on their mind. What problems and recommendations do they want to discuss?

Leaders who act like they are listening when they really aren't, lose credibility. Employees know when you're faking it.

Of course, the amount of time you spend talking and listening will vary from situation to situation. In general, the closer you get to a 50/50 ratio, the better.

The vast majority of people in my seminars and college classes have said that they need to spend more time listening and less time talking.

Read on to find out how others have found the right balance between being *talking* and *listening*.

What's your approach? Comments from the field

"I am a sales trainer who helps sales reps be more effective. What I teach sales reps regarding talking and listening also applies to leaders.

I recommend the 2:1 rule. You're most effective when you ask two questions for every one comment you make. This creates a two-way conversation. It serves much more as a dialogue than a monologue. You learn more about your people and then focus on what really matters to them.

You can assume you have people's attention for no more than 30 seconds without any input from them. Talk 60 seconds and longer, and you've lost them.

The key to hitting the talk/listen sweet spot has everything to do with focused awareness.

When you are keenly tuned in to your followers, you will learn how to best talk with and listen to them."

---Jeff Shore, President, and owner, Shore Consulting, Inc.

"Based on a suggestion from my leadership coach, I decided to talk less in meetings and even let there be some awkward silence. My staff, whom I had decided was extremely introverted, started to talk more. For extraverts like me, it's hard work, but it works. Try talking less and see what happens."

---Judy Zaiken, Corporate Vice President, LL Global, Inc.

"Listening can sometimes be difficult. Oftentimes it's because subordinates aren't presenting the information in a way that is geared towards my need to get to the heart of the issue from an ORGANIZATION-AL standpoint, not just a certain person's (or department's) perspective. My time constraints make me want to ask the direct, pointed questions on the topic and cut to making a decision on the answer.

It's important to realize this is not a 'cross-examination' while demanding yes and no answers. The other person can often add some nuance or explanation to the topic which can help with a better decision. That has to be balanced against the payoff though....at a certain point, limited information is good enough, and having a good decision is better than an exhaustive conversation with a perfect decision."

---Michael R. Matty, President, St. Germain Investment Management

Self-reflection

1. In what situations do you need to listen more and talk less?

2. How much time do you spend listening to customers, employees, suppliers, and experts in your industry?

3. In what situations do you need to state your view more clearly and concisely?

WORKING WITH THE TEAM AND WORKING ON THE TEAM

Do you spend more time working with your team or working on your team?

- ▶ **Working with the team** refers to engaging and interacting with team members to establish goals, develop plans, and make decisions.
- ▶ **Working on the team** refers to stepping back and assessing how well the overall team is working together and identifying specific actions to improve team performance.

Effective leaders help their teams work through various stages and learn how to work together in the most productive way.

Some team leaders spend all their time working with the team to get the task or project completed on-time and within budget. That's good but not enough.

It is equally important to spend some time working on the team. Some things to consider:

- ▶ Do all team members share in the team's mission, vision, goals, and values?
- ▶ Do all team members have the required skills and motivation?
- ▶ Do certain team processes (communicating, decision- making, conflict resolution, etc.) need to be improved?
- ▶ Do some team members need to be replaced?

Some leaders use "process checks" to get input from all team members.

At the end of a meeting, each team member does an assessment (excellent, good, average, needs improvement) of various factors related to teamwork such as:

- Staying on track (followed the agenda)
- Communicating (stated ideas clearly and succinctly)
- Listening (no side conversations)
- Making decisions (decisions were made in a timely manner)
- Assigning action items (clearly stated who needs to do what tasks by what deadline)

How team members evaluated each factor is then discussed. People who gave the item a high or low score make comments and discuss what worked well and what changes are needed to improve the next meeting.

How much time do you spend working on the team?

Read on to find out how others have found the right balance between *working with the team* and *on the team*.

What's your approach? Comments from the field.

"Working on the team—I use my experience and intuition to determine who is best suited to take the lead role in each situation. I believe in distributed leadership. There are many leaders on every team.

The cycles of business require different types of leadership. Entrepreneurs face this challenge. A start-up has different needs than a business that's grown to 100 employees. Each phase the business goes through presents new challenges to the leader. Being agile and flexible is vital."

---Dr. Rebecca Corbin, President, and CEO, NACCE (National Association for Community College Entrepreneurship)

"In my department, we have 10 teams that all do the same job. As a department, we determine our strategic initiatives and work on improving those for everyone. Examples: Creating a service and quality orientated culture (we are currently in a production orientated one), automating our work to be more efficient and increasing our mortality experience.

I lead two teams. I spend a lot of time working with each team. And, I work with individuals—coaching and mentoring them on ways to improve.

On occasion, I work on the team with the team. As a group we critique and discuss how well we are working together—communicating, problem solving etc. I probably need to spend more time on this side of the equation. It's important to step back on occasion and assess the quality and effectiveness of the teamwork."

---Neil Altieri, Director, New Business and Underwriting, MassMutual

"It is important to have the right balance of working with the team and working on the team. It depends on many factors such as the structure of the business, the number of team members, and the performance of both the individual team members and the overall team.

The stronger the team, the more opportunity you have to work with the team. The weaker the team, the more time you will spend working on the team. You need strong analytical skills and be a good psychologist. People are the most complicated resource you deal with."

---*Kate Dinobile, college student and former Bank Specialist at Sberbank of Russia*

Self-reflection

1. What actions can you take to improve your effectiveness in running meetings and working with your team?

2. What actions can you take to help your team improve its teamwork and overall productivity?

WORK LIFE AND FAMILY LIFE

How would you rate your work-life and family-life balance?

- ▸ **Work life** refers to the time and effort required to do your job and manage your career.
- ▸ **Family life** refers to the time and effort required to keep the household running smoothly, and spend quality time with family members.

Senior leaders have a dual role of being a parent to both their company and their family.

Work life is challenging and demanding. Executives are required to travel, attend important meetings, and be up-to-date on projects, people issues, and revenue goals.

Family life is also demanding. There is a long list of things that must be done, such as preparing meals, paying bills, doing laundry, and cleaning the bathroom. There is the extended family—attending family events and taking care of elderly parents is common these days.

When you add children into the mix, there is a variety of additional activities to schedule and attend.

It is important to build a strong family and a strong business. The two worlds overlap. Chaos and confusion in one area affects the other.

On a positive note, what you learn in one area may also help you in the other.

Some leaders overdo the workside of the equation. They work endless hours and have no personal life or spend little time with their family. This is not good—rather, it is awful!

Getting the work/family balance exactly right all the time is seemingly impossible.

Many leaders would admit it's always a work in progress.

Read on to find out what others think about the *work/life balance*.

What's your approach? Comments from the field

"I have a husband who travels for his job, three young boys, a dog, and a cat. They all have their needs and wants. And my work schedule requires some travel and some 'must attend' meetings.

The company culture needs to be supportive of the work/life balance. Allowing executives some flexibility in working remotely and juggling work hours as needed is helpful.

It's also important to have boundaries. You can't have your kids and family members calling and texting 15 times a day while you're at work. Nor should you have bosses and colleagues calling you at home during the dinner-homework-baths-making lunches for tomorrow period, except for emergencies.

At work or at home, I try to give whoever I am with my total, undivided attention. Be present--that's important."

> ---*Kate T. Labor, Vice President of Sales,*
> *System and Software*

"If someone could come up with a mathematical formula for the right work-life-balance, that person would become more famous than Lionel Messi. On a serious note, work-and-family-life balance is also a highly individual decision, and the right balance can only be determined by keeping the context in mind.

For a new mother, for instance, the balance may tilt more towards family, whereas a professional in his late 40s may want to spend more time at work and really scale that ladder of success.

You need to be sure of two things – A) What exactly do you want from life? B) Are you certain that you will not regret the choice you make later in life?

For example, you might decide that spending more time with family is important for you, but that would inevitably mean that your peers might get promoted faster or get better salary hikes or more strategic projects than you. Would you lament this decision 10 years down the line? If not, then you should certainly stick to the choice you have made. On the other hand, if you choose to make work your priority, you will inevitably have to miss out on watching your child perform at a school event. Can you make peace with the outcome of your decision?

These are questions that professionals have to ask themselves on an individual level, and there is no point in resenting the situation after making the decision. One lesson I have learned is that everything is a choice, and there are consequences for whatever choices I make. The ultimate decision is based on whether you are okay with a certain set of consequences as opposed to others. Make choices using whatever measure you find appropriate, and accept the consequences which come with the choice in order to lead a happy and fulfilled life."

---*Rostow Ravanan, CEO & MD, Mindtree*

Self-reflection

1. What actions can you take to improve your work life and family life balance?

SUMMARY-FINDING THE RIGHT RATIO

Leadership is far from an exact science. There is no magic formula that tells you what the perfect balance or blend is between two related leadership activities. You need to work at it! Keep learning and tweaking your approach to make the most positive impact.

Some suggestions:

- ▸ Ask your mentor what you could do more of and less of in specific situations
- ▸ Ask your colleagues for feedback
- ▸ Observe the ratios and approaches top leaders use in various situations
- ▸ Realize some situations are very unique and require a different combination of leadership actions
- ▸ Change your ratios as conditions change

The right ratio doesn't mean giving 50% of your attention to each leadership factor. Rather, it means finding the right amount of time and focus to give each factor, based on the current situation.

MOVE FROM BEING A GOOD LEADER TO A
GREAT LEADER!

ABOUT THE AUTHOR

Paul B. Thornton is an author, speaker, and adjunct professor of business administration.

He studied management, psychology, and political science at Ohio University. He was fortunate to take courses taught by Dr. Paul Hersey and Dr. Ken Blanchard. Their courses ignited his interest in learning what the best coaches, leaders, and managers do to help people grow, develop, and be their best.

Paul continued his education and earned an M.B.A. from American International College and a Master of Education degree from Suffolk University.

At age 27, he accepted a teaching and coaching position (varsity hockey) at American International College. His teams achieved a record of 63 wins, 33 losses, and 2 ties-- not bad!

After teaching and coaching for five years, Paul accepted a position at the Hamilton Standard division of United Technologies. He was directly involved in designing and delivering management and leadership training and development programs, succession planning, and many human resource initiatives.

In 1985 and 1996, he was the recipient of a United Technologies Award for Extraordinary Management Effectiveness.

While a professor of business administration at Springfield Technical Community College, he was the 2015 recipient of the Joseph J. Deliso, Sr., Endowed Chair.

Paul has published articles in *The Leader-to-Leader Journal, Engineering Manager, Management Review, Leadership Excellence, Electronic Engineering Times, The Toastmaster, USA Today*, and *The CEO Refresher*.

He is the author of 15 books including:

- ▸ *Precise Leaders Get Results* (Motivational Press)
- ▸ *Management-Principles and Practices* (Kendall-Hunt Publishers)
- ▸ *Leadership—Off the Wall* (Westbow Press)

Paul has created over 20 management and leadership videos that can be found on YouTube. He has published numerous slide presentations that are available on slideshare.net.

His wife, Mary Jean, is a talented leader, professor emeritus of business administration, and outstanding cook. They have two adult children: Kate (married to Corey) and Andy (married to Jess), and five grandsons: Anthony, Dominic, Keegan, Noah, and Owen. Future leaders—no doubt!

MY REQUEST

I would love to hear your story. What have you done to achieve your leadership sweet spot? What have you achieved when you operated in your sweet spot?

You can e-mail me at PThornton@stcc.edu.